I0446351

Talk Like a Pro

Talk to Anyone, Anywhere, Anytime

By

Gaby John

Disclaimer

Table of contents

Introduction

Have you ever experienced anxiety or awkwardness while interacting with a stranger? Have you ever found it difficult to maintain a conversation or leave a lasting impression? Have you ever wished you could speak with anybody, anywhere, at any time, more efficiently and confidently?

This book is for you if any of these questions apply to you.

Conversation: What is it?

A conversation is characterized as an informal discussion between two or more persons. Therefore, conversational skills are abilities we need to interact with others efficiently. Conversation skills, as opposed to written communication abilities, concentrate on our capacity for spoken communication. These abilities include the capacity to communicate ideas and meaning verbally as well as the ability to listen and comprehend what the other person in the discussion is saying. An essential component of socialization is learning how to have conversations.

Every day, we employ communication skills in a range of settings, including restaurants, stores, workplaces, and homes. These days, we use our phones, laptops, or tablets to hold virtual interactions with friends and family.

The Significance of Conversational Skills

Conversational skills are important because they enable us to establish rapport with others, carry out our objectives, and engage in productive interactions. Our happiness, self-worth, and confidence may all be impacted by our conversational abilities. Some experts claim that conversational skills are a blend of innate and taught qualities that allow us to interact, connect, and navigate with other people. In the social, professional, and personal spheres of life, conversational skills are crucial.

You will discover how to become an expert at having interesting and productive conversations by reading this book.

Proficiency in conversation is crucial not only for your social and personal life but also for your professional and career advancement. You can accomplish your objectives and create enduring connections using conversational skills, regardless of whether you want to network, convince, influence, bargain, or just connect with others. Having good conversational skills may also increase your happiness, confidence, and sense of self.

You'll learn how to avoid the mistakes that make most encounters go wrong as well as how to establish the tone, warm up, and prepare for every talk. Along with these skills, you will learn how to ask interesting questions, manage challenging discussions, conclude talks politely, and tell riveting tales.

You will be able to have better discussions and speak like an expert by the conclusion of this book.

Chapter 1

The Foundations of Effective Communication

The fundamental ideas and abilities that help us interact with others in a clear, accurate, and caring manner are known as the Fundamentals of Effective Communication. Some sources state that the Foundations of Effective Communication include:

- Listening intently and observing both verbal and nonverbal clues

- Controlling tension and emotions, and knowing when and how to express them.

- Speaking out and showing consideration for the thoughts and emotions of others.

- Modifying content and communication style to fit the audience and circumstance.

- Speaking in plain, succinct, and comprehensive terms; staying away from ambiguity and jargon.

- Avoiding criticizing and placing blame while using helpful and positive feedback.

- Making communication more remembered and engaging by using humor, anecdotes, and tales.

- Improving communication via body language, gestures, and visual assistance.

Chapter 2

How to Get Ready for Any Talk.

While some individuals find it difficult to strike up a conversation, others appear to have a natural ability to do so. Having the ability to strike up a conversation is an important social skill. Knowing how to start a conversation may make you feel more at ease and self-assured in a variety of social settings, whether you're trying to impress a prospective client, converse with a new friend, or get a date.

Being well-prepared for every discussion may provide you with the self-assurance and focus you need to handle a variety of situations with grace. Here is a useful primer to get you going:

Before the discussion:

1. Clearly state your goals and intended result.

Are you looking for information, offering criticism, or just chit-chatting? Being aware of your goal will enable you to keep the discussion on topic and focused.

What result are you hoping to attain? Determining the intended outcome will direct your strategy and assist you in gauging the effectiveness of the talk.

2. Investigate and compile data:

If there is anything special you need to know for the talk, find out ahead. This will provide you with pertinent information to back up your arguments.

If you're meeting someone for the first time, look into their hobbies or history to strike up a discussion.

3. Be prepared with possible subjects and inquiries:

Take into account the viewpoint and possible subjects that the other person may bring up. Get prepared with answers to frequently asked questions.

Make a list of icebreakers and conversation starters, particularly for first meetings.

4. Be prepared with possible subjects and inquiries:

Take into account the viewpoint and possible subjects that the other person may bring up. Get prepared with answers to frequently asked questions.

5. Control your feelings and thoughts:

Before the talk, give yourself some time to unwind and clear your mind. Breathe deeply or meditate to reduce anxiety and increase self-assurance.

Keep your spirits up and picture yourself having a productive discussion.

Watch Out for Conversation-Stoppers

Though it should go without saying, there are a few things you should never say until you know the other person really well. Even if your uncle often opens discussions at family gatherings with political commentary, gossip, complaints, and rude jokes, you shouldn't attempt to follow his example in your daily life. According to some studies, sticking with relatively harmless remarks can be your best option when it comes to conversation starters. In a research, participants were asked to rank the efficacy of a variety of starting statements that may be made by a possible love interest, including direct approach, open-ended, innocent queries, and sly "pick-up" lines.

The pick-up line strategy was not well-liked by respondents, although opinions on the other two opening techniques tended to be divided.

Men tended to be more upfront ("I'd like to buy you a drink!"), while women preferred to ask innocent queries like "What's your favorite team?"

How to Get Ready for a Discussion in a Group

The Dos and Don'ts

Tip: "Strengthen your argument, don't raise your voice."

A group of individuals known as participants in a group discussion, or GD as it is often known, exchange their thoughts and opinions with one another and work together to develop shared ideas to accomplish a common goal.
Information may be shared more easily in a group setting, where questions can be asked and answered and problems can be analyzed and solved by a team. A group conversation during an interview process helps a corporation narrow down the pool of potential applicants to a small number.

Taking part in the group discussion.

Let's first examine the prerequisites for group participation before delving into the specifics of the conversation. awareness of concerns, general information, and current events. Additionally, to participate in a technical group discussion, you must be knowledgeable about the topic at hand.

Goals or intention behind the group discussion:

- To create a shortlist of applicants for the next round of the hiring process.

- Evaluation of both technical and communicative abilities simultaneously.

- Obtaining new suggestions and ideas.

- Determine the issue's remedy or solutions.

Working in an organization needs a diversified workforce and employees who can work effectively as a team to create outcomes, which makes collaboration crucial. Group discussions are used in procedures ranging from recruiting to troubleshooting.

The group conversation goes through many stages.

- Orientation: The first round of talks in a group. The participants meet and wait for the instructions to be provided. The candidates are uncertain since they do not know who will start the conversation or serve as its facilitator. It's normal to have anxiousness and anxiety at this point in the group discussion. This sets the tone for the first talks on the topic. This phase involves discussing important milestones, choosing what has to be done next, and coming to a broad grasp of the participants and their perspectives.

You have a 50/50 probability of starting the conversation.

To capture and hold the interest of the team and the panel of judges, you will need to be well-versed in the topic, have accurate data, and possess strong communication skills. On the other hand, the panel and the team would both think less of you if you merely did it to be the first one to do it. Starting a conversation is an important activity that has to be approached carefully. In addition to numbers and facts, provide definitions, quotes, assertions, and stories.

- Conflict: When there are two or more parties engaged, a power struggle is unavoidable. Discussions in groups are no different. When tensions are at their highest, group members will confront one another with information and facts. When contentious topics are discussed, factions start to emerge, with some individuals endorsing and others opposing the viewpoints put out. Everyone will get embroiled in this heated argument as a result of this power struggle. The few who are aggressive, the dominating ones, the "YES" guys, and the passive players who don't add anything to the conversation are clearly distinguished from one another. When a contentious conversation is underway, it can go off track. The best course of action in this case is to remain calm and forceful.

In this phase, you may use both your creative and problem-solving abilities. Make an effort to include those who are not actively participating in the discourse.

- Teamwork: This is the cooperating stage. Upon determining the hierarchy, the participants transition to a composed and cooperative frame of mind. The group members start speaking honestly with one another, and disagreements may be settled quickly and easily. Here is when group conversation hits its peak in terms of information flow. Here, leadership abilities are still necessary. The players get an appreciation for one another's skills.

- Performance: The phase in which an individual showcases their abilities. In this stage, aptitude and attitude are evident. This stage involves evaluating abilities such as problem-solving, collaboration, and decision-making. Following a full conversation among all participants, a few common issues and solutions start to surface. The emphasis now turns to a thorough consideration of these chosen topics and the arguments against them. The group is motivated to reach their objective. Because of this, after a productive group debate, the members will often work together to arrive at the best logical answer without being forced to do so.

Tips for group discussions

o Make sure you are well-prepared and knowledgeable about the topic matter: Make notes on current events and the newest developments in the sector of your choice. Make an effort to commit some trivia and information to memory. Show off your vocabulary, but stay away from jargon unless it's correct, and don't use conversational language.

o Talk only when it is pertinent: Avoid cutting other people off during a presentation. Remain on topic at all times while debating with peers in a group setting.

o Take the lead: You can lead the group conversation. You will have an extra edge in a group discussion if you initiate the conversation. Make an impression to attract attention, but keep everything under check.

o Keep an eye out and practice active listening Pay attention to what other people are saying.

o Establish eye contact, then nod in acknowledgment.

o Develop your speech patterns and practice speaking in front of mirrors to help you communicate more effectively. Make sure that when you present your views, you don't hesitate or stutter.

o Body language: Your nonverbal clues have just as much weight. Avoid glaring and staring. Don't tap your fingers or slouch. Keep your head up and look them in the eye. When necessary, nod. Make sure your demeanor conveys your enthusiasm for being here.

o Don't intimidate allow others or take over the conversation. Allow people to make their arguments in a reasonable amount of time.

o Avoid being combative Avoid getting into debates solely for argumentation. Avoid yelling or raising your voice at other members of your team.

o Avoid playing both for and against teams. Make sure your ideas are cohesive. The majority of the subjects will be readily contested. Thus, choose whether you want to argue for or against the concept. Receiving feedback from both parties gives the false impression that you are not confident in your concept.

o Don't give up on speech time: While speaking up for a group discussion several times throughout the course is not required, don't settle for a minute and a half of speech time. Take the floor many times, restate the important ideas, provide your thoughts on other people's perspectives, and stay informed.

o Avoid getting caught up in the melee: During the group discussion, there will come a moment when everyone will speak at once. However, nobody will pay attention. Stay away from it. Raise your voice a little to make a statement in that cacophonous setting, and then finish off by sharing your thoughts.

o Group discussion facilitators: A facilitator's job is to encourage others to speak and bring out their expertise. A facilitator's job is to ensure that everything runs smoothly. In addition, the facilitator has to be impartial and possess in-depth topic understanding. The discussion should be continued by the facilitator, who must pose the appropriate question at the appropriate moment. In addition, the facilitator may need to pay attention to how the debate is going and ensure that it is fair. It is required of the group discussion session facilitators to be very skilled in summarizing and directing the discussion to the next subject. As a facilitator, they must maintain objectivity and guide the conversation without pressuring the group to reach a certain decision.

How can I take part in a debate in a group?

Prepare by going over the subjects and the accessible resources. Take a ton of notes and mark important points. Prepare any questions or remarks you would want to ask.

- Make an early arrival to convey your dedication. Having excellent time management skills will enable you to network with other attendees, manage your emotions, and project confidence.

- Speaking correctly: Stay away from tags and don't try to win them over. Don't doubt yourself by using qualifiers like "I think."

- Make use of the appropriate tone: Vary the volume of your voice and avoid boring them with repetition. Avoid coming out as too kind or severe. These elements all impact your credibility.

- Be courteous: Always give credit to those who have contributed to the team. After that, you are free to provide your interpretation and explain why it would be a preferable option.

Never minimize someone else's input into the conversation.

- Remain concentrated: Don't stray from the conversation's subject. Personally, you should refrain from going too far in the la-la world. Pay attention and listen well. Make sure the points are pertinent to the subject at hand, even if the discussion is still going on.

- Expand: Don't be afraid to add more points if you see that someone else is making the same arguments that you did.

- Body language: Make sure you talk with confidence and present an approachable, welcoming, and authoritative posture. Periodically make eye contact with the other members of the group. Avoid giving off the wrong impression by slouching, scowling, and fidgeting.

Chapter 3

Methods for Warming Up and Breaking Ice

Warming up includes small gestures like making eye contact and establishing rapport. You need to go a bit further in taking the conversation beyond light talk and forging a more genuine connection in order to break the ice. It is necessary to warm up and break the ice before striking up a discussion with a stranger or in a group situation. They might ease your anxiety, provide a welcoming environment, and foster rapport.

In Relationships

✓ Acknowledge your nervousness. Going on a date could make you feel more anxious than meeting someone in other situations for a variety of reasons! Acknowledging your nervousness in social situations or even on a first date could be a terrific approach to strike up a conversation. Since they are probably terrified too, just talking aloud what you both are thinking would greatly relieve the stress.

✓ Make a note of something about them, then communicate. Examine them closely, and record any thoughts you have regarding their look or demeanor. Pay attention to how they speak. Their speech pattern. Look to check whether they have anything especially spectacular, one-of-a-kind, or beautifully created. How do you feel about these findings?

Note: Physical remarks should be handled carefully since they could come across as false.

✓ Ask them to pose a question to you. Encouraging them to talk to you and ask questions can go a long way toward helping to break the ice in your budding friendship. "If you have anything you want to ask me, go ahead." For example, "If you want to ask about my wooden leg, it's okay. I can talk about it." could even be a better way to assist them.

✓ Adopt a direct approach. There's value in expressing your true feelings when it comes to matters of the heart. You might simply say to someone that you'd want to go on a date after getting to know them better. A break from the games can be a refreshing change of pace for most people, especially the more attractive ones, though some may find it off-putting. Say a phrase such as, "I apologize. I felt like I was going to lose my breath when I saw you across the room. I had to introduce myself or I would never be able to forgive myself."

- ✓ Remark on the name they have. Remark on their name and inquire about it if it is different from Sarah/John or if it is old, ethnic, or any other unusual combination. You can find out who they are named after, how their parents chose it if they approve of it, and other details.

- ✓ One of the most subtle yet effective methods to strike up a conversation with someone you don't know well is to ask them to settle a bet for you. How does it make you feel, for example, when someone says, "My friend says this outfit makes me look like Bill Cosby during his blue phase." or "According to everyone I know, boys won't even approach ladies who have short hair. How do you feel?"

At the office

- Asking someone you meet at work how they got to where they are is a great approach to start a discussion. You never know what kind of entertaining conversation you might have, as most people have really strange job trajectories!

- Find out about any honors or distinctions their company has recently gotten. If you conduct advanced research, you might find out about this kind of information. If they haven't worked for the company for a while, just make sure the accomplishment is reasonably recent so they will have something to talk about.

- Distribute a few Skittles. Pass a bowl of Skittles or another vibrant tiny candy around the room to break the ice with larger parties. Every time a candy piece is taken, the participant is required to answer a self-reflection question. The questions ought to be arranged according to the color of the candy; for example, a blue piece of candy would react to the question, "Where did you grow up?" The question "Which television program is your guilty pleasure of choice?" can have a green icon.

- Refresh your understanding of sports and popular culture. This may seem like a hassle if you do not like these things, but pop culture is the lowest common denominator by definition. You can read the entertainment and sports sections of the paper or the internet for a few minutes each day to get yourself ready for more chats.

- Look for mature approaches to break the ice. Usually, this entails showing up and striking up a discussion! Behave like an adult around your coworkers, partners, and other acquaintances. Game-based icebreakers are common in the workplace. A small percentage of people will usually find enjoyment in the games, but the majority will simply feel as though you're treating them like they're back in high school (since these kinds of games are so popular in classrooms). Making your partners or staff feel this way would be demeaning to them.

In Typical Social Situations

Pay them a compliment. Finding something about someone you actually admire or respect can help you strike up a discussion with someone you've never met before.

Just be sure to convey this admiration and respect in your voice. You can express your admiration for anything that comes to mind, including anything they've worked on, their personality, or their sense of style.

Perhaps anatomy isn't the best option after all!

- Be jovial. A nervous person may find it easier to relax and see that you're not scared if you act a little strange. If you are aware that people often perceive you as serious or threatening, use this strategy. Saying "Appletini," "Light on the little," or asking them what sign they are and then in a hilarious accent informing them of their horoscope are a few examples of how you could order a drink.

- Seek advice on good restaurants, places to visit, and things to do. The greatest way to persuade people to feel at ease and engage in conversation is typically to ask them to talk about something they enjoy. Act as though you're the new man. Declare in public that you're new or infrequently go out.

- Respond to the events occurring around you. If you pay attention to your surroundings, you'll soon find something to talk about. Something like building development, acts of generosity toward strangers, upcoming events, and architectural changes are all great starting points for a casual conversation with someone you've just met.

- One of the best ways to strike up a conversation is to ask someone to perform a tiny favor for you, such as holding a drink, keeping your place in line, reaching for something you can't reach, or giving you directions. Just make sure the assistance you're requesting won't take more than a few minutes of their time, and once they've finished, thank them and move on to a more relaxed discussion.

- In restaurants, coffee shops, and other establishments where food is served, you can strike up a conversation by inquiring about the person's drink or meal. You might ask them where they got it or what it is after complimenting them on how good it smells. After that, you can discuss the local cuisine, the item's special ingredients, etc.

What is the most effective icebreaker?

Find out if they are animal lovers or if they own any pets of their own. Since most people have pets, or even if they don't, they generally still enjoy having them, talking about pets is usually an excellent way to strike up a discussion.

Counsel

Asking them about their experiences or discussing your own painful ones should be avoided because they usually elicit negative emotions. You don't want to depress the other person right away when you strike up a conversation.

Chapter 4

How to Determine the Tone and Composition

Building rapport the act of connecting with another person via mutual trust, understanding, and harmony can lead to a stronger bond, better communication, and more cooperation. It entails reading the space and having the ability to make others feel at ease and comfortable with one another. To put it succinctly, rapport-building is the foundation of all meaningful connections. Building rapport with someone is similar to two perfectly fitting puzzle pieces coming together. We are able to connect on a deeper level and communicate easily. Without this base, relationships cannot grow and growth stagnates.

How Do We Build a Rapport?

- By being personable and putting newcomers at ease, you may open the door to improved communication and understanding with others.

- Active listening, being present, and exhibiting empathy are all necessary to show that you are genuinely trying to understand and connect with the other person. These are the initial stages of building a relationship.

- Distractions must be put aside in order to fully focus on the other person when you are present. Empathy demonstrates your concern for the sentiments of others and your readiness to place yourself in their situation. By showing that you appreciate the other person's viewpoint, active listening can foster a relationship based on mutual respect and understanding.

- Another strategy to establish rapport is to look for areas of commonality with the other person. Similar interests, pastimes, senses of humor, or life events can all be examples of shared experiences. Establishing a point of agreement can be a wonderful method to strike up a discussion and promote a feeling of community.

The Crucial Elements of Building Rapport

Rapport-building talents are the strategies and tactics people employ to create a harmonious connection with others and assist people in creating more meaningful and productive encounters in both personal and professional contexts.

In order to build rapport, you must be sincere and real. When you do, others will sense it and be more likely to connect and trust you. Being genuine is being true to yourself, being forthright and honest, and exhibiting a readiness to hear and understand other people's points of view. Having patience is another essential for developing a relationship. Strong relationships take time to establish, so it's crucial to exercise patience and let things happen organically. In fact, rushing the procedure can make you appear dishonest and hinder the development of rapport. By listening intently, being present, showing empathy, finding common ground, imitating behavior, projecting energy and optimism, and being honest and patient, you may forge enduring relationships with people . Crucial elements needed to build rapport are:

1. Being Aware

Studies have indicated that attentive listening can strengthen bonds between people and facilitate dialogue.

It means showing the other person that you genuinely care about what they have to say and offering them your whole attention. By adopting methods like keeping eye contact, nodding, and giving verbal feedback, you can demonstrate that you are understanding and paying attention.

2. Gratitude

Empathy, which is the capacity to understand and experience another person's feelings, is shown to be a critical component of both successful relationships and communication. Putting oneself in another person's shoes and honoring their feelings are key components of empathy.

3. Genuineness and Sincerity

Being real and truthful in your interactions with people involves staying true to who you are and not trying to be someone you're not.

Authenticity and honesty have been associated with improved trust and healthier relationships in both personal and professional settings.

4. The Appropriate Handle

According to research, touch can improve social interactions, fortify relationships, and even lessen stress and anxiety when it is handled sensibly and properly. When utilizing touch as a strategy to establish a connection, keep in mind personal boundaries and cultural variations. Touch has the ability to convey intimacy, warmth, and trust, forging a feeling of proximity and connection.

5. Trying to Comprehend One Another

Identifying similarities between the other person's hobbies, interests, or life experiences can help foster a feeling of connection and rapport.

According to studies, resemblance is the basis of attraction, leading to more pleasurable interactions and closer relationships.

6. Positive Attitude

Happy and positive attitudes can help build rapport fast and give a great first impression. People are drawn to folks who are cheerful and positive because positive feelings are contagious.

7. Inside Are Jokes and Humor

Studies show that sharing laughter makes people feel more relaxed and connected, which fosters stronger bonds and partnerships. Since they create a shared experience and foster a sense of trust and understanding, humor and inside jokes also aid in rapport-building.

8. Being mindful

Building mutual understanding and trust can be facilitated by keeping an open mind and being attentive to the ideas and opinions of others. Research indicates that maintaining an open mind enhances relationships, reduces conflict, and facilitates better communication.

Is It Possible To Get Along With Someone Quickly?

There are practical methods to expedite the process of building rapport with a new individual, but it can frequently be slowed down. One such tactic is "behavior mirroring," which involves subtly imitating the other person's movements, voice tone, and body language. By making the other person feel at ease and known, mirroring fosters a relationship that is particularly beneficial in romantic and flirtatious situations.

By being optimistic, you can establish a strong relationship and leave a lasting impression. Because enthusiasm is contagious and people are more inclined to feel the same way, being upbeat and enthusiastic is also a wonderful approach to building rapport quickly.

How to Be Nice to People When Interviewing for a Job

Building a strong rapport with the interviewer is crucial because it could improve your chances of getting the job. Here are some strategies to help you do this:

1. Analyze the company

If you take the time to learn about the firm and are familiar with its vision, values, and culture, it will show that you are genuinely interested in the position and that you are prepared. It is also important for you to be aware of its latest news, significant achievements, and goods and services.

2. Show ardor

Be zealous and positive the entire interview. Making eye contact, grinning, and speaking pleasantly will convey your excitement for the opportunity. Additionally, you want to discuss how your qualifications and experiences fit the job requirements and the company's values.

3. Engage in Active Listening

By engaging in small talk, nodding in agreement, keeping eye contact, and using vocal cues like "yes" or "I understand" to demonstrate that you are interested in the interview and the information being shared, you can demonstrate that you are paying attention.

4. Call the interviewer's name.

Use the interviewer's name to build rapport and demonstrate that you are listening during the interview.

You might also try calling them by name occasionally to demonstrate your want to get to know them better.

5. Seek out areas of consensus

By pointing out shared experiences or interests, you might establish a rapport with the interviewer. Establishing a common interest, hobby, or connection can foster a positive relationship and enhance the overall interest and the quality of the talk.

6. Be truthful.

Be genuine and authentic in your responses; avoid giving prepared answers; share personal anecdotes and examples that highlight your qualifications for the position by showcasing your abilities, experiences, and values. This will help the interviewer get a better idea of who you are and how you would fit into the company culture.

7. Understand the Body Language You Employ

Your body language plays a big part in developing a rapport. To show curiosity, keep your arms relaxed and open, and slant slightly inward. As much as you can, attempt to read the interviewer's body language to establish a sense of mutual understanding and connection.

8. Thank the interviewer.

After the interview, thank the interviewer for their time and thoughtfulness and say how much you appreciate the opportunity to talk about the role and your interest in the organization. By expressing your gratitude and interest in the role in a handwritten note or follow-up email, you can further cement the rapport you've developed during the interview.

9. After Your Interview

Allow yourself some time to reflect on the interview, including how you did, the questions posed, and any comments made. Make a list of the things you did well and the things you could improve upon for the next interview.

Consider following up with an email within a day of the interview to let the interviewer know you're interested in the position and to thank them once again for their time. This email can also be used to respond to any follow-up queries you might have had or to elaborate on any topics that were not thoroughly discussed during the interview. In addition to being courteous and professional, this email follow-up makes you more memorable to the interviewer.

If you are not selected for the current position, use professional networking sites such as LinkedIn to stay in contact with the interviewer and the employer. This will support you in keeping the relationship you established during the interview and might potentially open doors for you in the future.

Inquire about helpful criticism of your performance and suggestions for future interviews. This demonstrates your dedication to both professional and personal growth, which can make a good impression on the interviewer and possibly lead to future chances with the organization. Consider this an opportunity to improve yourself in the event that you receive comments or learn that you were not chosen for the post.

How to Build Strong Working Relationships

Building rapport with teammates and coworkers requires cultivating strong relationships with supervisors, stakeholders, and coworkers.

The following are some methods for building rapport at work:

1. Be affable

When engaging in social interactions, ensure that your posture is comfortable and your arms remain uncrossed to convey a friendly attitude. Make sure to extend a kind greeting and use their name to build a personal rapport. Be personable, cordial, and transparent. Make eye contact and smile.

2. Consciously pay attention

Avoiding outside distractions, focusing entirely on the speaker, and providing both verbal and nonverbal feedback are all examples of practicing active listening. To demonstrate your understanding of the speaker's point and your participation in the discourse, summarize or paraphrase what they have said. Pay attention to what other people are saying, and when you ask questions, express your interest in their thoughts and perspectives.

3. Display Empathy

Relationships can be strengthened and trust established by putting oneself in other people's shoes, trying to understand their perspective, being sensitive to their feelings, and showing compassion when things are tough.

4. Seek out areas of consensus

By deciding on shared interests, hobbies, or life experiences, you can establish common ground with others. Establishing a sense of belonging within the group, building personal connections, and engaging in talks about common interests can facilitate rapport-building and enhance teamwork and collaboration.

5. Make Use of Powerful Communication

When arguments come up, deal with them politely and concentrate on coming up with a solution rather than using strong language or making personal attacks. Communicate succinctly and clearly, and be considerate of other people's viewpoints. Be receptive to criticism and engage in active listening.

6. Cooperate with one another

Work together to achieve attainable objectives and be prepared to offer credit when credit is due. Be open to fresh perspectives and prepared to compromise when needed. Encourage candid dialogue among team members and allow them a forum to express their views.

7. Thank you.

To promote a positive work atmosphere, recognize individual achievement as well as team accomplishments. Thank people for their efforts and acknowledge and appreciate their contributions. Say "thank you" as often as possible and in a timely way. You may also show your gratitude with modest gestures of appreciation or with written letters.

8. Possess Credibility

Establish trust by acting in a straightforward, honest, and consistent manner; by taking responsibility for your mistakes and owning up to them; by keeping your word; and, where required, by maintaining confidentiality.

9. Keep an optimistic attitude

Maintain an optimistic attitude and look for opportunities to support and uplift people. Congratulate others on a job well done and, if needed, provide constructive criticism. To foster a pleasant work environment, recognize and celebrate successes, focus on finding solutions rather than issues, and support a growth attitude.

How to Encourage Employees to Build Positive Relationships with Customers

Building a good rapport with clients is crucial to providing a satisfying customer experience, which may increase client loyalty and encourage repeat business. As a manager or employer, you can encourage your employees to establish a positive relationship with clients by:

1. Setting Objectives

Make it clear to your staff that the organization values and prioritizes building rapport with customers. Specify clear parameters for customer service and rapport-building exercises, and share these goals frequently.

2. Providing Guidance

By providing regular support and resources such as role-playing exercises, workshops, or access to customer service professionals, employees can enhance their rapport-building abilities. Provide instruction and direction on how to establish rapport with clients by using empathy, active listening, and finding points of agreement.

3. Providing a Positive Example

Having a positive relationship with customers is one way that you, as an employer, can lead by example for your employees. You can accomplish this by maintaining a cheerful attitude, addressing issues in a professional manner, and showing a sincere interest in finding out about the wants and worries of your clients.

4. Recognizing and Respecting Successful Relationship Building

Reward and acknowledge employees who have built rapport with clients. This can be achieved by highlighting their achievements in corporate newsletters, telling success stories in team meetings, or offering rewards like bonuses, extra time off, or gift cards. By doing this, you may motivate employees to keep improving their rapport-building techniques.

5. Creating a Positive Work Environment

Promote open communication, cooperation, and a caring atmosphere where staff members are at ease discussing their experiences and picking up tips from one another. In your contacts with customers, stress the value of empathy, active listening, and establishing common ground. Create an environment at work where providing excellent customer service is valued and where staff are encouraged to go above and beyond to establish rapport with clients.

6. Providing Opportunities for Recommendations

Use questionnaires, comment cards, or face-to-face interactions to get feedback. Give your staff a copy of the feedback, emphasizing their successes and outlining areas for development. Make use of the comments to guide future training and development initiatives. Invite clients to tell your staff about their experiences. Make use of the feedback to identify and enhance your rapport-building abilities.

7. Promoting Collaboration

Give staff members chances to work together through cross-functional projects, brainstorming meetings, and team-building exercises. Promote the exchange of success stories, best practices, and lessons gained among staff members to improve their ability to establish rapport with clients. Encourage staff members to collaborate and exchange approaches for establishing rapport with clients in order to promote a culture of ongoing learning and development.

Chapter 5

How to Tell Captivating Stories

You Have Stories to Tell

Your life is made up of tales, not because you're exceptional. But since everyone's life is essentially a succession of tales. If you've ever thought to yourself, "Yeah, but I don't have any great stories to tell," you're mistaken. But before we go any further, let's address this one question: what is a story?

A tale is a sequence of confrontations that finish in a takeout. Every writer and story strategist has a distinct understanding of the term "story." (And we're all a touch pedantic and contentious about our definitions.) But no matter what your definition, storytelling, at its root, is a technique for expressing the importance of human effort.

You work and struggle, conquering hurdles. Finally, you either win or lose that victory or loss results in a takeaway, which is the sole objective of any tale.

Without the takeaway, you don't have a significant tale.

Did you catch the keyword there? Meaningful. You might have a tale with lots of tension, but if you don't offer your audience a takeaway, it loses purpose. We care about tales because we want to feel the sigh of relief that comes with encountering lived knowledge. We're waiting for the takeout. We know it's coming, and it had better be there in the end.

The Ancient Greek's Stories Aren't So Meaningful Anymore

The legends of Ancient Greece are no longer significant to most contemporary individuals. (Except for oddball academics.) Make sure your tales are important to your AUDIENCE, not just to yourself.

Why Bother Telling A Story?

Aside from giving folks a dopamine boost, what's the objective of telling a story?

Stories are how we humans prefer to learn and arrange knowledge. We'd rather be given a narrative with a takeaway than be taught that we must think or behave a particular way. We'd rather be told a tale than offered a pile of features and perks on a sales page. You may utilize narrative in commercial and political speeches, sales pages, website text, and emails that truly sell. You may utilize storytelling at cocktail parties, in the classroom, and anytime you deal with folks prone to being distracted or bored. Now then, let's share some tales!

How to Tell a Story

If you want to simply share tales during public speaking or socializing with friends, use these 12 storytelling strategies.

- Open your tale with something unexpected that draws your audience's interest.

- Read the room to ensure it's a suitable moment to tell your tale.

- Use speech to bring the characters to life.

- Pay attention to your audience to see which parts of the tale are landing.

- Play with your voice and timing to generate drama.

- Don't be hesitant to speak with your hands while you tell your narrative.

- Keep the story moving ahead by concentrating on what comes next.

- Share what you or the main character were thinking throughout important occasions.

- Tell a couple of different individuals the same tale and alter it each time.

- Watch comedians deliver tales and pick up their timing tactics.

- Build your plot towards a major dramatic moment.

- Finish with a payout that offers folks a giggle or an aha moment.

How to Tell a Story Well

There are a few things that every excellent story must possess. Whether you're developing a short film, composing a sales email, or attempting to woo a new client, your tale has to include these major story elements:

Main Story Elements

1. Main Character

2. Objective or Desire – What does your character want?

3. Obstacles – What external and internal difficulties come in the way? What hinders your character from attaining what they want?

4. Big Moment of Epic Conflict i.e. a kicker, or the straw that broke the camel's back. — This may not be essential for an anecdote, but for a lengthier tale, it's helpful. I call this moment the Vader Face-Off because you can see it so clearly in the Star Wars movies as Darth and Luke face off at the climax of the film. This is the main moment of the Epic Conflict.

5. Win/Lose Moment – Does your character receive what they want? Or do they fail? You may have an up ending or a down ending depending on what you're attempting to communicate.

6. Takeaway – What did your character learn from this?

7. Final Transformation – How has your character changed today compared to before going through this struggle?

The Life Before & The Call Create Contrast and Capture Attention

There are two last plot parts that I feel are very necessary: Life Before and The Call. Not every quickie narrative incorporates them, but I believe that they should. These factors are intricately related. So here's how you utilize these two elements:

The Life Before & The Call

Describe what your character's Normal Life is like before they receive The Call that changes everything. The call isn't necessarily a real "call." Though you'll discover it frequently is. It's the time your character is prompted to take action either by themselves or by a supporting character or guide. It's frequently more potent to have the call be external. The character is frequently hesitant to answer the phone. She doesn't want to change. She's not sure whether she can go forward. She's frightened of failure. But then…something shifts inside of her, and she chooses to heed the call.

Example of the life before/the call.

This is the tale of how absolute vanity saved my life:

When I was in my early 20s, I slipped into an existential despair. I smoked cigarettes, drank cheap red wine by the cupful, and ate bowls of Cool Whip at 2 in the morning. I loathed myself, but I wouldn't do anything to make a difference since I honestly felt that I would die at any time, so any activity was meaningless. I can recall lying in bed gazing up a the ceiling, seeing a yawning abyss of darkness slowly rolling over my existence. It seemed like the Edvard Munch Scream painting was taking over my thoughts.

Then something occurred.

But it's not what you may assume. I got a massive zit. I mean, it was red, furious, and roughly 1 centimeter in diameter. It was the King Kong of zits. It perched on my temple, and it refused to depart. Week after week, it remained there. Finally, one day as I stood in the bathroom staring at myself in the mirror, I thought, "I'm going to get rid of this zit, no matter what it takes." I instantly got ready and did what I usually did when I needed a solution: I went to the bookshop.

That's the beginning of a lengthier tale of how I eventually overcame depression.

The Life Before was my useless life. I was facing an existential crisis. The Call was this stupid zit coming up on my face. It wouldn't go away, and I was forced to make a choice. I was forced into action.

NOTE: This narrative is not a genuine life story, it's simply to offer an example so you can understand better.

The Call provokes a character to take action, despite their hesitation. If you can integrate the Life Before and The Call in your tale, you'll provide your viewers with a more rewarding experience. You'll also be giving them a clear indication that they're going to hear a narrative. As you start speaking about the Life-Before moments, your audience understands that they're going to hear a narrative. As soon as they hear The Call, they settle in.

They know that there's going to be a Takeaway, and they commit to hearing your tale.

3 Storytelling Tips

1. Make sure your story is relevant.

Choose a tale that's relevant to the difficulty your audience is facing.

It's not that you can only tell tales about companies if you're writing to company owners. Or that you can only tell tales about acting if are writing to actors. Instead, make sure that the takeaway is relevant to the challenges your audience encounters. That stated, the more your tales are packed with individuals your audience can connect to the better. You'll be more inclined to assist them in realizing what's feasible for them.

2. Make sure your story is meaningful.

There must be a takeout.

You can't tell a tale that has no key takeaway. While you're doing it, try to choose tales that you think are especially significant. My depression story is significant to me. It makes me feel something. It lights up my spirit. When you're intrigued and inspired by a narrative, it transmits better to your audience.

3. Make sure you've got enough conflict to power a lengthy story.

You don't need to tell grandiose tales.

They may be a few phrases. The longer you go, the more conflict you require. For a small product page imagine you're selling a lip balm you may have an exceedingly brief tale. It doesn't need to be pages lengthy.

You can use Tale for anything.

From an e-commerce product listing to a financial advisor's website, narrative can assist ideal clients and consumers in understanding why what you offer should matter to them.

Chapter 6

How to Handle Difficult Conversations

Why is addressing uncomfortable talks important?

Here are some reasons it's crucial to manage unpleasant talks properly in the workplace:

- ✓ It might boost your work satisfaction.

- ✓ It may help you create better ties with coworkers.

- ✓ If you're a manager, it may guarantee your team members feel more appreciated.

- ✓ It may help you enhance your productivity.

13 techniques for handling uncomfortable discussions successfully

When participating in a challenging discussion at work, it's crucial to regulate your emotions, use cautious language, and concentrate on developing solutions with which both sides feel comfortable. Considering these general aims, here are 13 suggestions to consider before having an uncomfortable conversation:

1. Have the talk as soon as possible

Putting off uncomfortable talks might make you feel more apprehensive over time and increase the stakes for a conversation. Therefore, when expecting a hard topic, attempt to participate in it as soon as you can rather than avoid it. Engaging in discourse in a timely way might assist you in offering a rationale for having the conversation. It may also prevent difficulties from escalating and hurting other members of the team.

2. Determine the aims of the talk

As you approach a challenging discussion, attempt to first determine your objectives in having it. Consider what you want to accomplish in the discussion and what tactics you may employ to reach this objective. This way, you may feel prepared to engage in the discussion and steer it with confidence. You could make a list of speaking points before the talk to assist you in keeping calm and focused on your aims.

3. Choose an appropriate location for the talk

Before you establish a meeting time for a hard talk, attempt to identify a good venue for it. Consider holding the talk in a neutral location like a conference room or a coffee shop where both sides feel comfortable sharing space. Even more, if you fear the topic could escalate, having a chat in a public location might help you prevent any emotional escalations.

4. Listen with an open mind

It's possible you're approaching a hard debate with conflicting opinions. Therefore, try to retain an open mind while you connect with them. They may provide an explanation that simplifies the situation for you and helps both of you handle the issue more readily. Consider using active listening skills, such as paraphrasing what the other person has said to ensure you get their meaning.

5. Offer empathy

Both of you may be concerned about initiating a tough subject, and these sorts of talks often provoke emotional reactions. With this, it's crucial to be able to show empathy to your partner throughout and reassure them that you're having the talk with the intention of achieving a resolution. You may exercise empathy during hard interactions by picturing what the other person could be experiencing.

6. Use resolution-oriented thinking

Most challenging talks begin with the objective of establishing a resolution. Try to retain this aim as an anchor throughout your chat and prevent letting the subject fall into pointless debate. From here, you may work together to find a resolution that works for both of you. If the other person consents, you could take notes throughout the chat, so you can construct a solution that fulfills all of your requirements.

7. Speak using first-person language

Try to employ sentences that begin with first-person language rather than second-person language. This helps you to constructively explain your own opinion and avoid accusing words. By doing so, you may find it simpler to participate in a critical conversation comfortably. For example, you may express how you feel or what challenges you're having owing to an issue.

8. Use ad rem tactics

Ad rem conversational tactics enable speakers to concentrate on addressing the pertinent facts of a situation rather than indulging in personal assaults. Therefore, employing these tactics will help you accept ownership for your role in a circumstance, evaluate what went wrong, and analyze any repercussions honestly. From here, your discussion partner may be more open to your views.

9. Ask questions and practice active listening

As you begin your talk, accept that you may have predetermined assumptions about a topic. In your discussion, you may overcome any of these beliefs by asking your partner questions about their viewpoint and how they understood the topic at hand. This may assist you in obtaining a better grasp of what their requirements are and how you two can coordinate to create solutions.

10. Manage your emotions

Any feelings you experience during a challenging talk are certainly real and it's probable you may start to feel despair, worry, or rage. Despite this, it's crucial to notice your feelings inwardly and moderate your responses to prevent escalating the topic. Conversely, if the other person begins to overtly express similar emotions, assist them in regulating their emotions by identifying their sentiments and treating them with respect.

11. Be confident in your viewpoint

As you talk about your opinion, attempt to do it directly and confidently. Being confirmed in your views and ideas might assist the other person in noticing that you've thought deeply about the matter and better grasp what your aims are. This strategy might be particularly helpful if the other person disagrees with your opinion and seeks to discount it.

12. Know when to take a break

In the thick of a challenging discussion, it might be hard to know when to take a break. Despite this, when the debate begins to emotionally escalate or gets circular, it's necessary for you to take a step back to protect your mental welfare and examine different ways to the problem. Taking distance after a heated debate might help you recharge and prepare to interact more carefully going ahead.

13. Establish a follow-up procedure

While the aim of a tough discussion is to leave it with an agreed-upon conclusion and happy sentiments, this doesn't always occur. Sometimes, conversation partners need time to recuperate emotionally after hard talks and may have to take distance from one another to reestablish their connection.

Therefore, when you finish a session, set a plan for following up with the other person at a later date to check on them and verify the resolution you made together.

Common conversational blunders and How to Avoid them.

Some typical conversational blunders and ways to prevent them are:

- Interrupting others: This might make the other person feel insulted, ignored, or annoyed. To prevent this, wait for your turn to talk, and utilize verbal or nonverbal indicators to communicate that you want to say anything. You may also apologize if you mistakenly interrupt someone and let them continue their argument.

- Rambling: This might cause the other person to lose interest, feel bored, or get confused. To prevent this, be precise, succinct, and focused on your topic. Use a structure, such as a primary point, supporting information, and a conclusion. You may also check in with the other individual to see if they are following you and ask for comments or questions.

- Repeating the same thoughts over and again in the same conversation: This might make the other person feel frustrated, impatient, or misunderstood. To prevent this, make sure you have a clear purpose and aim for the talk. If you feel that you are not getting your point across, attempt to reword it or use a new example. You might also ask the other person to explain or repeat what they learned from you.

- Talking over others: This might make the other person feel belittled, insulted, or frightened.

To prevent this, respect the other person's right to speak and listen carefully. If you disagree with anything, wait until they finish and then share your view gently and constructively. You may also recognize their point of view and strive to establish common ground or compromise.

- Being excessively verbose and taking over the conversation: This might make the other person feel excluded, irrelevant, or overwhelmed. To prevent this, be careful of the time and the balance of the discussion. Give the other individual an opportunity to talk and participate. You may also offer open-ended questions, show attention, and encourage them to express their ideas and emotions.

- Glancing at your mobile phone during conversations: This might make the other person feel disrespectful, distracted, or disinterested. To prevent this, put your phone aside or on quiet mode while you are having a conversation.

If you need to check your phone for an urgent issue, excuse yourself and explain why. You may also apologize and restart the discussion as quickly as feasible.

Chapter 7

How to End Conversations Gracefully

Have you ever been in a discussion when there reaches a lull, and both participants simply disengage from the conversation and walk away? Ending a discussion may often be difficult. Or maybe it's a circumstance where you need to depart, but the other person simply doesn't grasp it. They keep chatting and talking, and you want to go, but you need to do so in a gracious manner. It doesn't have to be embarrassing. Here are a few suggestions for quitting a discussion gently.

The Basic Exit

It doesn't take much to depart. You may say something like:

✓ It was good to meet you. Thanks for talking.

Or

✓ I've got to go. Talk to you later.

Something along those lines can work. Depending on who it is and the subject, it may be an easy way to depart the conversation.

Give a Reason

You may also mention a reason why you need to leave.

✓ It was wonderful chatting with you. I'm going to/need to go socialize a bit/meet some other people/get some snacks/go to the bathroom/check out some of the other exhibits/(and the list goes on). Talk to you later.

One component in presenting a cause to depart a discussion is that it has to be real and you actually need to do it. Otherwise, the other person may feel that you lied to them and feel upset or jilted.

Express appreciation

Another method to terminate a discussion is to express gratitude for anything that the other person said or done.

- ✓ I appreciate you helping me grasp "X". I've had to leave, however. Talk to you later.

- ✓ Thanks for sharing that tale with me. I need to go locate Bob. Talk to you later.

- ✓ Thanks for the positive message. I truly need it. I need to leave now, however. See ya.

Give a Positive Remark or Reflection

You may also make a good comment or reflection from the chat to depart.

- ✓ It was extremely lovely to meet you. I appreciated hearing about the story with the cat. Haha, hilarious. Talk to you shortly!

- ✓ That was amazing hearing about your narrative about your mountain climbing adventure. I need to go, however. Talk to you later.

- ✓ Good luck in the competition tomorrow. I'm confident you will do amazing. I need to head. Let me know how it goes!

Exchange details (if applicable)

If it's someone you recently met and would want to chat with again, you may exchange details as part of your departure.

- ✓ Thanks for the talk. I need to leave, however, Could I obtain your contact data and speak later?

- ✓ I loved conversing with you. Could I obtain your number and chat with you later?

- ✓ I've had to leave, but if you give me your email address, I'll hit you up later.

Suggest a future meeting (if applicable)

You may also propose a meeting in the future.

- ✓ Hey, I've had to leave, but I would love to hear more about your experience. Maybe we could meet up anytime next week?

- ✓ It was good chatting with you, but I've had to get off. A number of us are gathering at the coffee shop next week. Want to join us?

When someone won't catch the clue

Sometimes people are domineering and won't let you go, while other times folks are merely lonely and hate to lose a listening ear. Either way, there are instances when someone won't let you go. You may still depart gracefully and properly.

- o Be firm: When the speaker continues talking or adds, "One more thing", stay firm. Tell them again that you truly have to leave.

- o Interrupt: Normally it's not nice to interrupt. But in this situation, it is alright. If the speaker continues chatting, you may stop them again and say something like "I really have to go. Talk to you later".

- o Use the proper body language: Make sure that everything in your body language suggests that the talk has ended and you have to depart. When the individual won't catch the message, point your body and feet away from the person as if to go off.

o Just say excuse me and go away: If they still don't get the clue and you've told them you have to go many times, you may simply have to leave. Look at the person, say excuse me, and then walk away.

Example 1:

You: It was lovely chatting with you, but I've had to go speak to Frank. See you later.

Person: Wait, I didn't tell you about the time that I went to the park and…

You: I would love to hear it another time, but I really need to go speak to Frank. I'll catch you later.

Example 2:

Person: It was wonderful, I saw this enormous elephant that...

You (pointing body away from the person, maybe even glancing to where you want to go some): I've had to go, see you.

Person: No wait, there was this red balloon that was circling around...

You: Excuse me (and walk off).

Exiting a discussion doesn't have to be hard. If you follow these criteria, whether you want to simply go simple, provide a reason, express thanks or a good comment, or ask to exchange data or for a future encounter, you may depart properly and graciously.

Conclusion

In this book, you have learned how to master the techniques of successful and entertaining communication. You have learned how to prepare, warm up, and establish the tone for every discussion, and how to avoid the mistakes that spoil most relationships. You have also learned how to deliver interesting tales, listen attentively and empathetically, ask intriguing questions, manage challenging discussions, and terminate talks graciously.

By practicing these abilities, you will be able to communicate like a pro and experience the rewards of better discussions. You will be able to connect, engage, and inspire your audience, whether they are your colleagues, clients, friends, or strangers. You will also be able to enhance your relationships, collaboration, problem-solving, and general social and emotional well-being.

However, mastering these abilities is not enough. You also need to practice them routinely and consistently. The more you practice, the more confident and comfortable you will become in diverse social settings. You will also be able to adjust and improvise according to the individual and the circumstance.

Remember, talking is an art that can be learned and developed. It is also a gift that may be shared and appreciated. So, don't be hesitant to start a discussion, join a chat, or prolong a conversation. You never know what you may learn, discover, or experience from a discussion.

Thank you for reading this book and accompanying me on this trip.

I hope you have found it informative, interesting, and amusing. I also hope you will utilize what you have learned to make your talks more meaningful and memorable.

Kindly leave a review if you learnt a lot from this book and you are confident that you can communicate effectively like a pro.

Now, go ahead and speak like a pro. Talk to anybody, anywhere, anytime. And have a nice talk.